D0353385

It's not fair

New contact details:
School Libraries
Resources Service
Phone 020 8359 3931
Fax 020 8201 3018
slrs@barnet.gov.uk

HODDER
Wayland

a 30131 03926439 2

LONDON BOROUGH OF BARNET

Your Feelings

I'm lonely   I'm happy
I'm worried   I'm special
It's not fair I feel bullied
I'm shy

First published in 1997 by
Wayland Publishers Ltd

This edition published in 2001 by Hodder Wayland,
an imprint of Hodder Children's books
Reprinted in 2002 and 2003

© Hodder Wayland 1997

Series editor: Alex Woolf
Designer: Jean Wheeler

British Library Cataloguing in Publication Data
Moses, Brian, 1950-
It's not fair. - (Your feelings)
1.Fairness - Juvenile literature 2.Justice - Juvenile literature
1.Title 11.Gordon, Mike 1948-
170

ISBN 0-7502-2132-1

Typeset by Jean Wheeler
Printed in Hong Kong

LONDON BOROUGH OF BARNET SCHOOL LIBRARIES RESOURCES SERVICE	
21-Feb-05	PETERS
152.4	£4.99

It's not fair

Written by Brian Moses

Illustrated by Mike Gordon

HODDER
Wayland

an imprint of Hodder Children's Books

When something isn't fair...

I feel like a bee that can't reach a flower...

I feel like a big cat trapped behind bars...

I feel like hitting out at someone.

When something isn't fair...

I march out of
the room...

SQUEAK!

SLAM!

I slam the door...

I stomp up the stairs.

When my big sister gets some expensive trainers and I don't...

it's not fair.

I need new trainers too, Mum!

When my friend gets taken to the cinema to see the latest cartoon film but my Dad won't take me...

it's not fair.

When everyone else is picked to play football and I'm not...

it's not fair.

And I even scored a goal
in the last match!

When everyone else is allowed to go on the big slide at the funfair and I'm not...

it's not fair.

YOU HAVE TO BE THIS TALL TO RIDE THE SLIDE!

'You can go on the slide when you're older.' That's what my parents say.

When my brother won't let me have a go on the computer, even though he knows it's my turn...

it's not fair.

'Let me have a go
or I'll SCREAM!'

Eeeeeeeeee!

Even grown-ups sometimes think life isn't fair...

Why don't I ever win the lottery? It just isn't fair.

19

When I say 'it's not fair',
Dad says I should be
thankful for what
I've got.

'When I was a lad...' he starts off.
And then he tells me just how
little he had!

Sometimes I can see that I'm better off than someone else.

My big sister thinks it isn't fair when she has to do homework and I don't.

My friends all say I'm lucky when we go on holiday to France.

It's **n̲o̲t̲** fair!

I know my dog thinks it isn't fair when we all go out for the day and leave him in the house.

I can tell from the
sad look on his face.

When was the last time you heard someone say, 'It's not fair'?

Perhaps that someone was you.

Notes for parents and teachers

Read the book with children either individually or in groups. Ask them to think of situations when they felt something wasn't fair. Which of the ideas on pages 4 and 5 is closest to how they feel, or do they picture themselves in different ways? Can they illustrate how they feel?

Children might like to write a story based on an occasion when they felt something wasn't fair. Remind them that they don't have to stick with the truth in a story. Something that happened to them could just be a starting point and after that they can resolve the situation in any way they like. If children are stuck for an idea they could use one of the 'It's not fair' situations in the book. What happens when your brother/sister won't let you have your turn on the computer? What happens when you sneak off to have a go on the fairground slide?

Encourage children to write short poems with the repeating phrase 'It's not fair...' They could be addressed to a brother or sister:

> When you get new shoes and I don't,
> it's not fair.
> When you're allowed to stay up late and I'm not,
> it's not fair.

When you always get first pick of the sweets,
it's not fair.

Children might enjoy acting out 'it's not fair' situations.
Ask them to suggest starting points and see what develops.
Other children can comment on whether what they saw
acted out was realistic or not. How else might the situation
have been resolved?

Talk about whether children always show fairness to others
themselves. Who will admit to being unfair occasionally?

Are there situations when everyone would agree that something isn't fair? Can children think what these kind of
occasions might be? They might include name-calling,
bullying, racism, favouritism, foul play, crime or cruelty
to animals. Do children have strong views about some of
these issues?

Explore the notion of fairness further through the sharing
of picture books mentioned in the book list on page 32.

The above ideas will help to satisfy a number of attainment
targets in the National Curriculum Guidelines for English
at Key Stage 1.

Books to read

Here's Kitty! by Bel Mooney (Mammoth, 1992). A set of short stories about a small girl called Kitty and the various times when she thinks that life isn't fair.

Farmer Duck written by Martin Waddell, illustrated by Helen Oxenbury (Walker Books, 1995). It isn't fair that the farmer stays in bed all day while his duck does all the work around the farm. The other farm animals decide to teach the farmer a lesson. A lovely book about justice and fair play.

The Second Princess by Hiawyn Oram and Tony Ross (Collins Picture Lions, 1995). The Second Princess thinks it isn't fair that she should come second all the time and she thinks of ways in which she might get rid of her sister. Fortunately she soon finds out that everyone can come first – some of the time.

Good Girl, Gracie Growler by Hilda Offen (Happy Cat Books, 2000). Gracie Growler has a new baby brother. Everyone pays him lots of attention and it just isn't fair how nobody seems to notice what Gracie does any more!